MY FIRST LOOK AT SEASONS

THE LAND COMES ALIVE WITH COLOR IN SUMMER

Summer

JILL KALZ

CREATIVE EDUCATION

Published by Creative Education

123 South Broad Street, Mankato, Minnesota 56001

Creative Education is an imprint of The Creative Company

Designed by Rita Marshall

Photographs by Barbara Augello, Dennis Frates, Getty Images (John Marshall, B. Anthony

Stewart/National Geographic), Tom Stack & Associates (John Gerlach, Joe McDonald,

Milton Rand, Inga Spence, Mark Allen Stack)

Cover illustration © 1996 Roberto Innocenti

Printed in the United States of America

Library of Congress Cataloging-in-Publication Data

Kalz, Jill. Summer / by Jill Kalz.

p. cm. — (My first look at seasons)

ISBN 1-58341-364-2

1. Summer—Juvenile literature. I. Title.

QB637.6.K35 2004   508.2—dc22   2004056249

First edition 9 8 7 6 5 4 3 2 1

Summer

The Hot Sun

June is here! The sun feels hot. The grass is green. Many people go on vacation. In the northern half of the world, June 21 is the first day of summer.

Summer days are the longest and hottest of the year. The sun rises early each morning and sets late each night. The sun feels hottest around lunchtime.

JUNE 21 IS THE SUNNIEST DAY OF THE YEAR

Sometimes, summer air feels "sticky." Sticky air is called humidity. Humidity makes a hot summer day feel even hotter.

Summer storms can be dangerous. Lightning flashes. Thunder rumbles. Windy storms called tornadoes spin across the land.

THUNDERSTORMS BRING CLOUDS AND LOTS OF RAIN

Green Everywhere

Summer is growing time. Bright, hot summer days help plants grow. Rain helps, too. Farmers' fields turn green in summer. So do trees, bushes, and other plants.

Trees make food in their leaves. When trees are making food, their leaves look green. Some trees make fruit, too. Apples, oranges, and lemons grow on trees. So do peaches and pears.

THE SUMMER SUN HELPS TOMATOES GROW

BUTTERFLIES FEED ON SUMMER FLOWERS

Summer flowers come in many colors, shapes, and sizes. Bees help plants make flowers. They carry **pollen** from plant to plant on their legs. Plants use the pollen to make flowers.

Living in the Heat

Animals have a lot of food to eat in summer. Many birds eat worms and seeds. Deer and rabbits eat grass and other green plants. Foxes and snakes eat mice.

Sometimes, very hot temperatures

last for many days.

This is called a heat wave.

The summer sun can be very hot, so many animals sleep during the day. Mice, owls, and bats sleep until the sun sets. Frogs stay out of the sun, too. The sun dries out their skin.

Some animals love the sun. Butterflies open their wings and warm themselves. The sun gives them energy. Lizards and snakes get energy from the sun, too.

Ants are common summer insects.

So are flies, mosquitoes,

beetles, and bees.

FROGS JUMP INTO WATER TO COOL OFF

People sweat when they are hot. Sweat helps keep people cool. Dogs pant when they are hot. Rabbits stay cool by losing heat through their long ears.

A Fun Season

Many people do things outside in summer. They swim, fish, or play tennis. They go biking or just lie in the sun.

Dogs and other animals drink a
lot of water in summer. This
helps them beat the heat.

Some kids go to summer camp. Camp is a place to learn new things and make new friends. Camp may last a few days or all summer. Many families go on vacation in summer. Others go to fairs. On the **Fourth of July** and **Canada Day**, some people light fireworks.

Summer is a fun **season**. Enjoy it! Pick flowers! Jump into a pool! Watch a baseball game! And then, get ready for fall!

A drought happens
when no rain falls
for a long time.
Plants dry out and die.

Hands-on: Frozen Bananas

Too hot outside? Beat the heat with these cool treats!

What You Need

Two firm, peeled bananas, cut in half

Four popsicle sticks

One cup (240 ml) melted chocolate chips

One cup (240 ml) candy sprinkles

A paper plate

A plastic knife

Wax paper

What You Do

1. Put the sprinkles on the plate.
2. Carefully push a popsicle stick halfway into the cut end of each banana.
3. Spread chocolate evenly over the bananas, then roll them in the sprinkles.
4. Place the bananas on a piece of wax paper. Freeze them for two hours. Then enjoy!

BANANAS AND OTHER FRUITS NEED SUMMER RAIN

Index

Words to Know

Canada Day—July 1, a day that celebrates the country of Canada

Fourth of July—a day that celebrates America's freedom

pollen—fine yellow powder that flowers need to bloom

seasons—the four parts of a year: spring, summer, fall, and winter

Read More

Branley, Franklyn Mansfield. *Tornado Alert.* New York: HarperCollins Children's Books, 1990.

Chapman, Gillian. *Summer.* Austin, Tex.: Steck-Vaughn, 1997.

Thayer, Tanya. *Summer.* Minneapolis: Lerner Publishing Group, 2001.

Explore the Web

Enchanted Learning: Activities and Crafts for July 4th

http://www.enchantedlearning.com/crafts/july4

Kids Domain: Summer

http://www.kidsdomain.com/holiday/summer

Rainbow Magic: Summer

http://www.rainbow-magic.com/holidays/summer